A Scrumptious Sundae

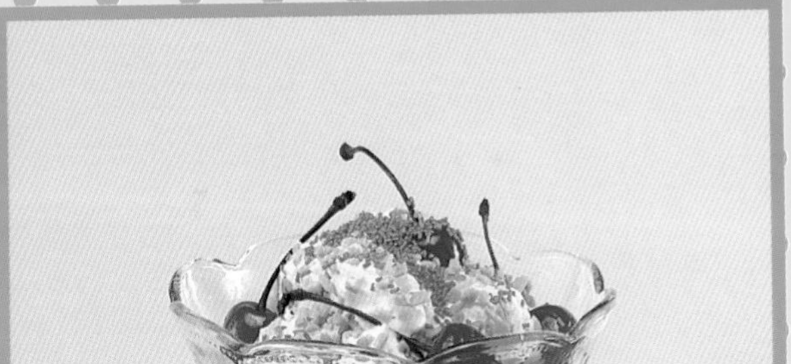

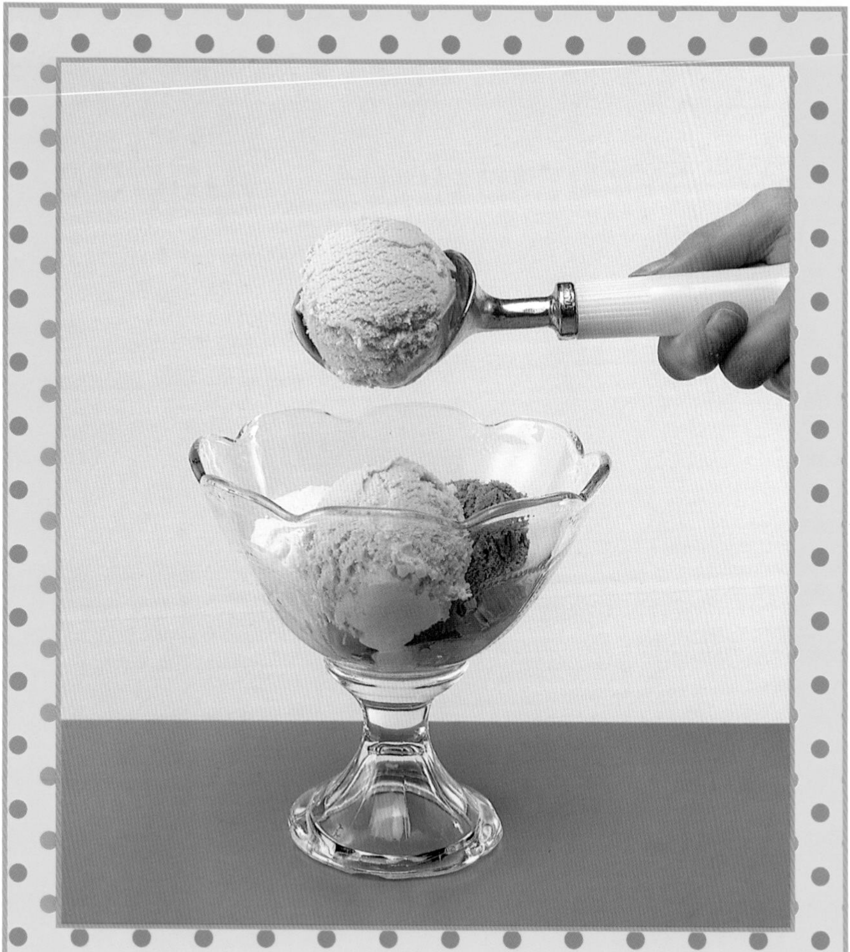

Some ice cream,

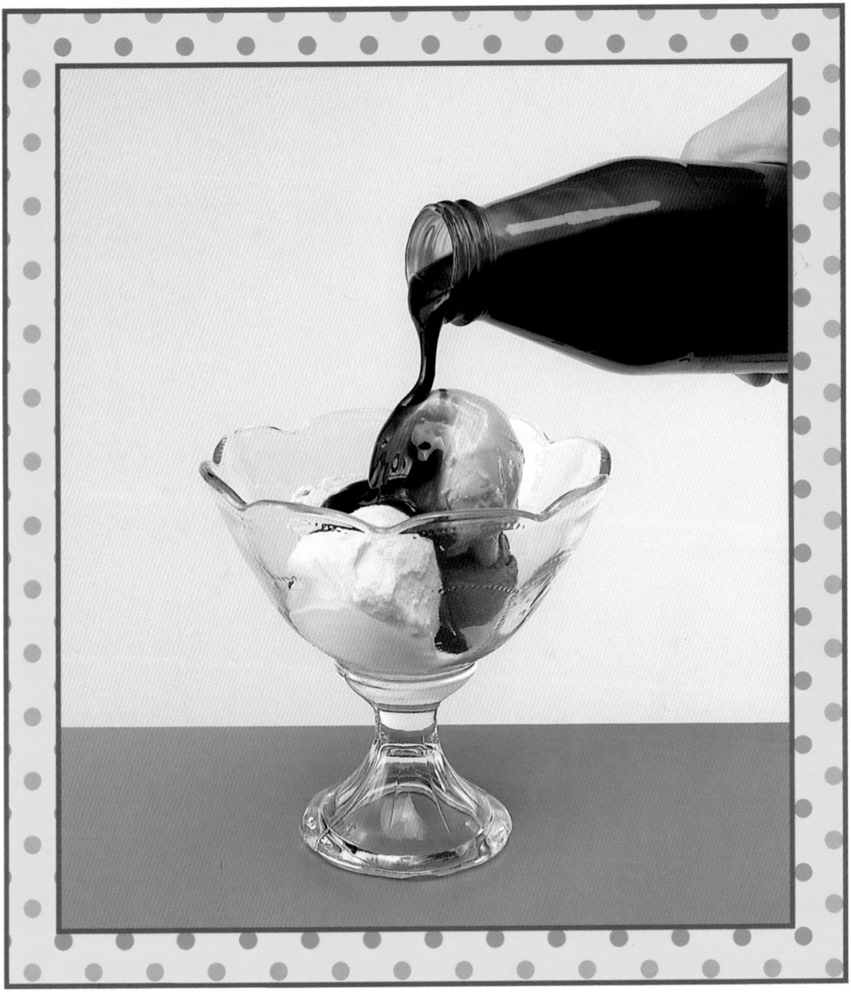

some chocolate sauce,

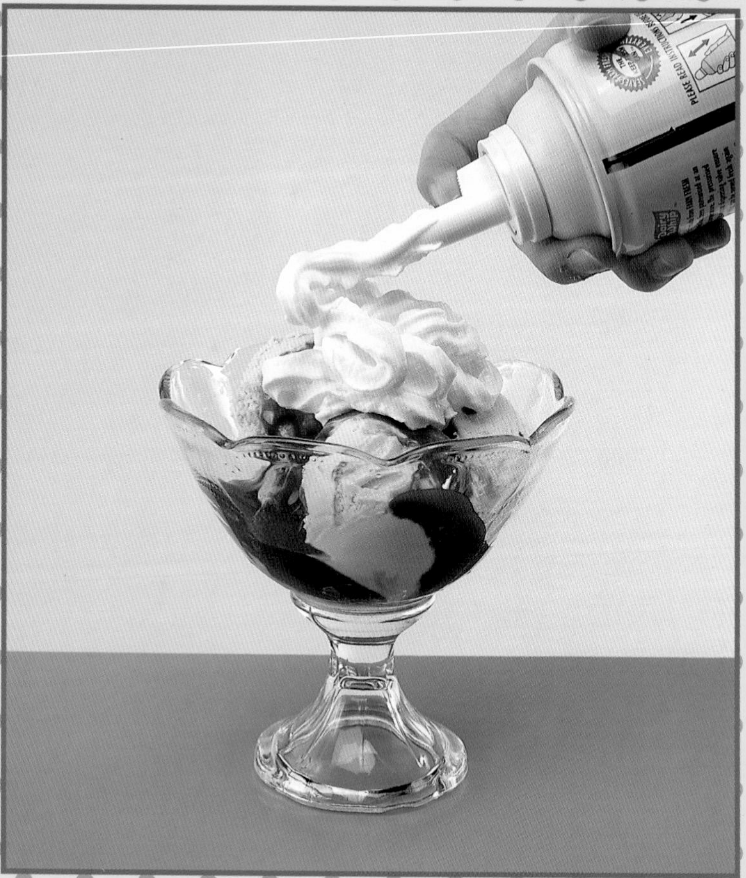

some cream,

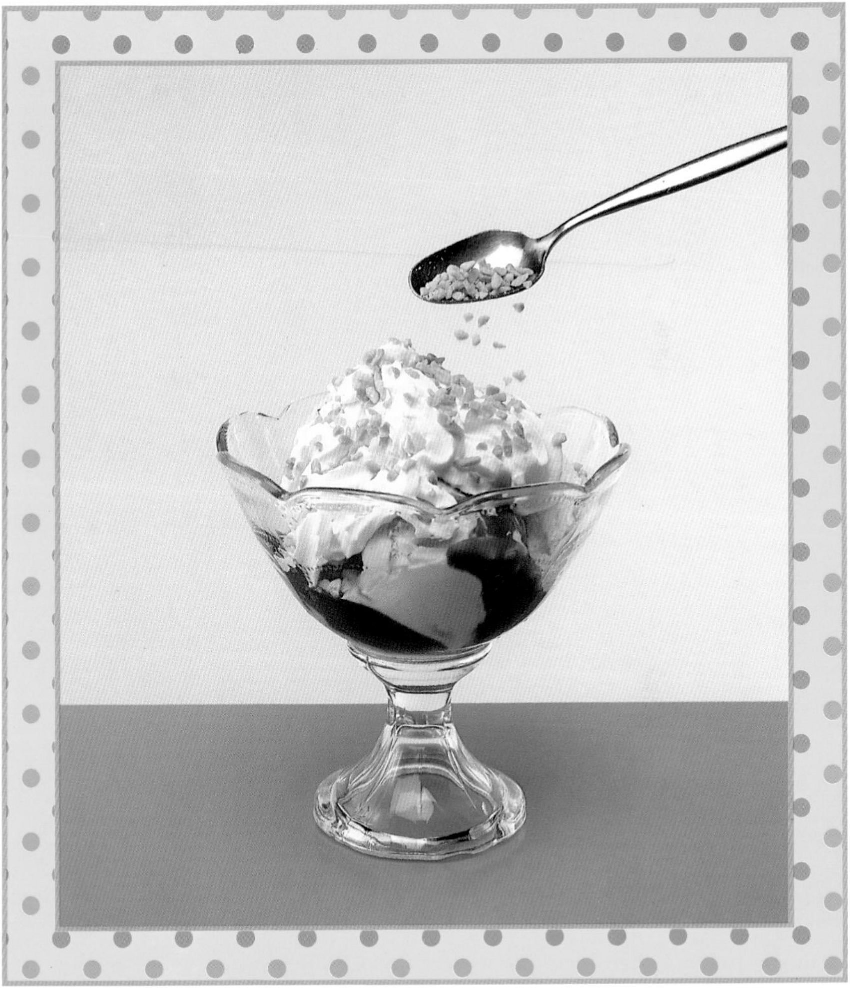

some nuts,

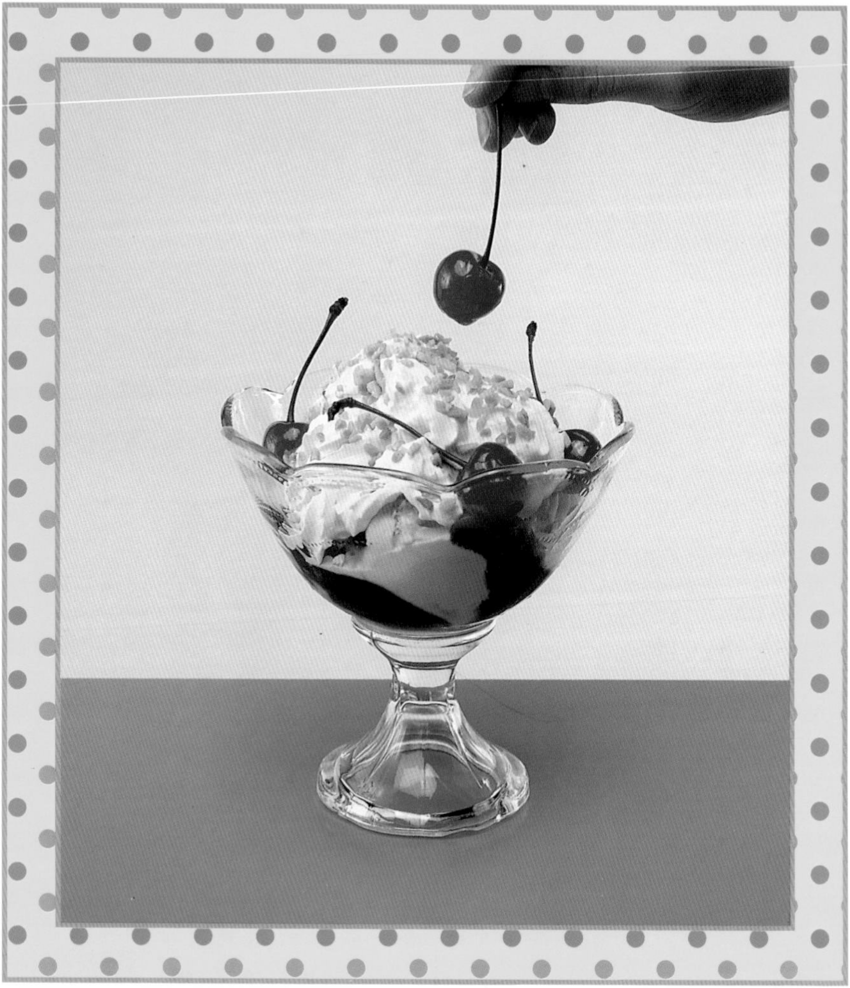

some cherries,

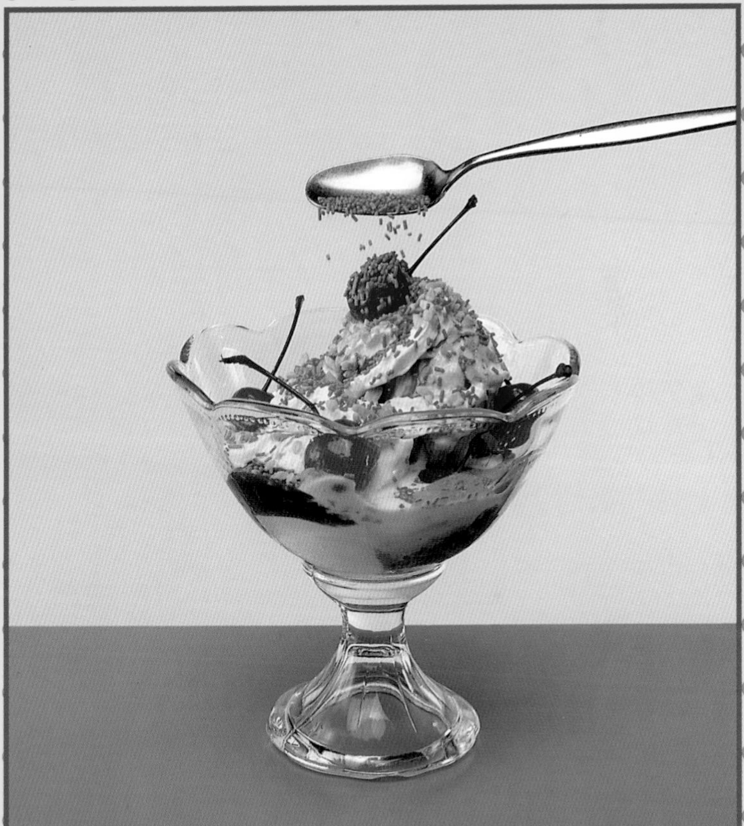

some sprinkles...

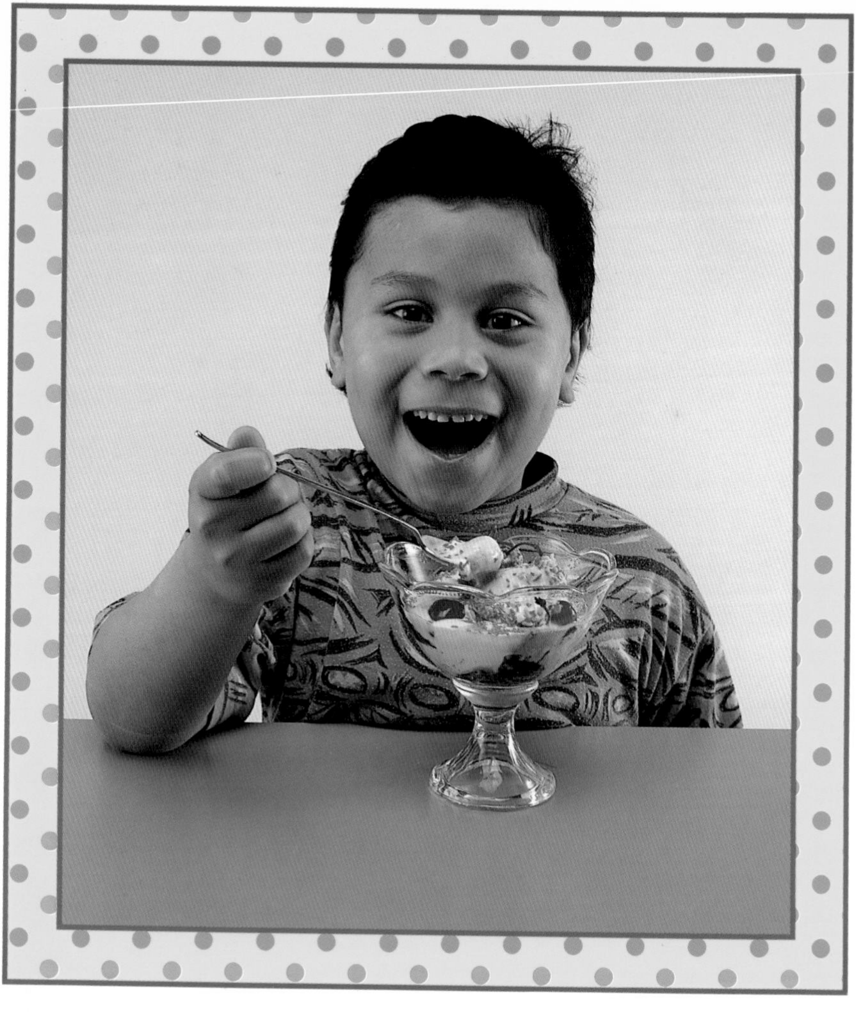

a scrumptious sundae.